Things

TO DO

WITH

Dad

WRITTEN BY CHRIS STEVENS
ILLUSTRATED BY A.J. GARCES
(WITH ADDITIONAL ILLUSTRATIONS BY DAVID WOODROFFE)

EDITED BY RACHEL CARTER
DESIGNED BY ZOE QUAYLE

Things TO DO WITH Dad

Lots of Fun for Everyone

SCHOLASTIC INC.

New York   Toronto   London   Auckland   Sydney
Mexico City   New Delhi   Hong Kong   Buenos Aires

Stevens, Chris, 1964-
Things to do with dad : lots of fun for everyone / written by Chris Stevens; illustrated by A.J. Garces; with additional illustrations by David Woodroffe; edited by Rachel Carter; designed by Zoe Quayle.
  p. cm.
ISBN-13: 978-0-545-13402-6
ISBN-10: 0-545-13402-1
1. Recreation—Juvenile literature.   2. Amusements—Juvenile literature.
3. Play—Juvenile literature.   4. Father and child—Juvenile literature.
I. Carter, Rachel.   II. Garces, A. J., ill.   III. Woodroffe, David, ill.   IV. Title.
GV182.9.S74 2008
790.1'91—dc22   2008039866

First published in Great Britain in 2008 by Michael O'Mara Books Limited,
9 Lion Yard, Tremadoc Road, London SW4 7NQ, United Kingdom.
www.mombooks.com

Cover design by Angie Allison
Cover illustration by Paul Moran

12 11 10 9 8 7 6 5 4 3 2 1   9 10 11 12 13 14/0

Printed in the U.S.A.
First American edition, April 2009

 # Contents

Introduction

Free time is ten times more fun when it is shared. Whatever games and activities you dream up, they take on a whole new meaning when Dad and the kids get involved. So whether it's the weekend, the holidays, or that precious free hour at the end of a busy day, here are dozens of ideas for activities that will have everyone grinning from ear to ear.

If you've got energy to burn, this book contains sports and games ideas to exercise both mind and muscles. If it's new toys you want, there are all sorts of ingenious and inexpensive playthings to make within these pages. If you need ideas for indoor fun, there's lots to do when it's raining outside. And if you want to sneak a little education into playtime, you'll even find a few facts hidden among the fun.

There are hand symbols throughout to ensure fingers get muddy and sticky but not hurt.

 This symbol indicates tasks that are best carried out by Dad, such as using matches and sharp tools.

 This symbol is for tasks that kids will particularly enjoy.

So, what are you waiting for? It's "Dad-time" . . . make the most of it!

Turn Your Kitchen into Dad's Diner

Feeling hungry? Don't head to a fast-food restaurant when you can cook up a delicious and nutritious feast in your own kitchen. Homemade burgers taste great and are inexpensive to make, and mind-blowing milk shakes can be whipped up in an instant.

THE MOST AMAZING BURGERS IN THE WORLD

For four large burgers you will need:

- 1 small onion
- 3 cloves garlic
- 1 egg
- 1 pound lean beef
- 1 teaspoon chopped thyme
- 1 teaspoon chopped parsley
- a pinch of salt and pepper

- a generous splash of tomato sauce
  - olive oil
  - 4 burger buns

For the garnish you will need:

- 2 scallions
- chopped lettuce, radishes, and raw onion
  - sliced pickles
  - ketchup
  - mustard

GET COOKING

 Finely chop the onion and the garlic.

 Crack the egg into a large bowl and beat it with a fork.

Put the meat in a large bowl. Using a wooden spoon, mix in the egg and the onion. As you stir, add the garlic, herbs, salt and pepper, and the tomato sauce. Then use clean fingers to combine the mix.

Put the mixture onto a chopping board and roll it into a slab just about 1/2 inch thick.

Divide the slab into four pieces and shape each one into a disk with your hands. Don't squeeze them into balls though, they have to stay flat.

Coat the bottom of a frying pan with olive oil. Heat the oil until it is really hot, before adding the raw burgers. Fry the burgers on each side for five minutes or until cooked through.

Tip from Dad: For added flavor, thinly slice some cheddar cheese. Place the cheese on top of the cooked burgers and lightly grill until the cheese starts to bubble.

THE SHOWDOWN

Place each burger on a bun.

 Now it's time to get creative. Garnish the top of each burger with the sliced scallions. Then add chopped lettuce, radishes, raw onion, sliced pickles, ketchup, and/or mustard.

GREAT SHAKES

Banana and chocolate milk shakes make the perfect burger accompaniments. So go ahead, place your order.

For each person you will need:
- half a glass of skim milk
- 3 tablespoons of chocolate syrup
- a ripe chopped banana
- 1/2 teaspoon vanilla extract
- straws

Pour the milk into a blender and add the chocolate syrup. Make sure the cover is properly secured, then start the blender on a low speed.

When the two are thoroughly mixed, switch off the blender and add the banana and vanilla extract.

Blend again until the shake looks creamy and delicious.

Pour the milk shake into a tall glass and put a straw in it.

Tip from Dad: Instead of adding banana to the mix, if you're feeling adventurous, try a dollop of peanut butter. Or, leave out the chocolate syrup and add a handful of strawberries with the banana.

For the final touch, decorate paper napkins with "DD" in big capital letters. That's the logo for "Dad's Diner." Next stop, "DD" restaurants worldwide!

Create a Crazy Golf Course

Guess what? Your home is a crazy golf green just waiting to happen, and you're guaranteed free membership to this course.

All the materials you'll need to build the course are within arm's reach. The aim of the game is to knock the ball into a saucepan or frying pan — but first you have to hit tricky targets and find your way around all kinds of obstacles.

Half the fun of this game is designing the course and steering clear of its traps.

You will need:

- a long umbrella, a cane, or a hockey stick to use as your golf club • saucepans and/or frying pans
- lots of obstacles, such as books and tin cans
- a tennis ball

SAFE-TEE TIPS

Before you tee off, hide anything breakable. It is a good idea to use a tennis ball instead of a real golf ball, but stay away from rooms with expensive, fragile objects, such as TVs. When you are playing, remember to tap the ball lightly — it makes your stroke much more accurate.

A COURSE IN DESIGN

Now you're ready to set up a series of challenging holes. Use a combination of objects such as tin cans, books, shoes, and rows of toy cars, or try building these holes:

The CD Challenge: Zigzag between pairs of CD covers balanced on their sides, but don't knock any over!

The Bathtub Bunker: The bathroom course starts in the bathtub, now renamed the bunker. Instead of trying to play your way out of the bath by hitting the ball straight up the side, try aiming for the end opposite the faucet

Tin Can Alley: Tin cans make great building blocks for bridges and tunnels. Before the ball lands in a hole, hit it through a series of tin-can bridges in the right order. If you miss a bridge, you have to go back to the start.

Roll Up, Roll Up: The ball must travel through a triangular tunnel of books, roll down an avenue of toy cars, slip between two shoes without touching them, and roll up another book into a saucepan.

You don't need to build *all* your holes. Why not put one under a bed? If you have stairs, make them a central part of your course. Tell players they must hit the ball down the stairs and into an awaiting saucepan.

Old pieces of plastic gutters are great for hitting the ball onto chairs or around tight corners.

MARVELOUS MARBLE GOLF

If space is tight, try playing desktop crazy golf using a marble as a ball. Hit it with a pencil through a maze of books and toys, or flick it with a fingertip along a path of rulers and cardboard tubes.

WHAT'S THE SCORE?

However you play, keep count of the number of times each player hits the ball before finishing the course. Add five penalty points to this score whenever obstacles are missed or knocked down.

Once all the players have completed the course, the player with the lowest score wins.

Turn a Tin Can into a Lantern

For a seriously spooky Halloween party or a magical outdoor barbecue, glowing lanterns are a must-have.

Here's how to make a fantastic lantern from an empty tin can.

You will need:

• a marker • a clean, empty tin can (the type that is opened with a ring-pull is best as it is less likely to have a sharp edge) • a hammer • nails • a wire coat hanger • wire cutters • a pair of pliers • a candle

Using the marker, draw a pattern of dots on the can. You could draw a skull and crossbones, hearts and diamonds, or a firework starburst. Let your imagination run wild.

Mark two big dots on opposite sides of the can just below the top edge. These mark the position of the holes you will use to attach the wire handle.

Fill the can with water to the brim and carefully stand it upright in the freezer. The water in the can must turn into a solid lump of ice because this will prevent the can from buckling when you start punching holes in it. Be prepared to wait at least twenty-four hours for the water to freeze completely.

When it's ready, place the can on a firm surface, such as a workbench, and bang a nail into the side through one of the dots. Then use the pliers to carefully pull the nail out of the can, leaving a hole. Try using different-sized nails to make holes of varying size.

Repeat this process until you've made all the holes.

Now stand the can in a bowl of warm water until you can remove the ice.

To make the handle, cut a length of wire from the coat hanger and bend it into a U-shape. Hook the wire through the holes at the top of the can, and bend the ends over with the pliers to secure them.

Dry out your lantern and put an unlit candle inside it (the holes on the inside will be jagged, so watch your fingers). Light the candle carefully.

Watch with wonder as the light shines through the holes.

Build a Snow Fort

Snowmen are so last season! Instead, build a snow fort. This will give you a huge sense of satisfaction and put Dad's do-it-yourself snow skills to the test. Best of all, you'll end up with a secure base for staging the most awesome snowball fight ever.

You will need:

- lots of snow
- a long stick
- a large square or rectangular plastic mold, such as a recycling box or storage box
- 3 pieces of wood for door supports
- 1 piece of board for window supports
- a scarf and a short stick • an old blanket

Optional:

- some fun-shaped molds
- a piece of sturdy board that is big enough to make a platform to stand on

BUILDING TECHNIQUES

Look around for a prime spot to build the fort. You are looking for flat ground, in an open space, with a plentiful supply of deep snow. Mark out the base of your fort by dragging the stick through the snow to make a large square or circle.

Fill the mold with snow, stamping it down as you go. When the snow is tightly packed, carefully turn the mold over and stamp on the base of the box to release your first snow brick.

Repeat this process until you have enough bricks to mark out the base of the fort. Don't forget to leave space for the door.

Join the bricks together by pressing snow into the gaps between each one, just like the mortar in a brick wall.

 If necessary, use a kitchen knife to cut the snow bricks to size.

Next, put a layer of snow on top of the first row of bricks before building the second tier. Make sure each new brick overlaps the bricks on the row below, rather than lining up with them.

When the fort is three bricks high, dig a small hole on either side of the doorway. Push a wooden door support into each hole so that it stands upright. Check that each support is deeply rooted in the snow, so that it will stay in place.

Leave a gap for a window, so you can spy on your snowballing enemies. Before building a layer of bricks on top of the window, lay the window support board across the gap.

Once the walls are high enough, rest the last door support across the space you have left for the door. This will support the layer of bricks that are laid on top.

Add more layers until the fort is high enough to act as a shield against sneaky snowballs, but low enough for you to see over.

FINISHING TOUCHES

Tie a scarf to a stick to make a flag. Carefully push your flag into the top of the fort wall. Lay an old blanket on the floor of the fort.

 Find a pile of snow and make a stash of snowballs. Take some snowballs into the fort and line them up on the fort wall. Leave a few outside for the fort's attackers.

Let the snowball fight begin!

Tip from Dad: For a really impressive fort, make a step that you can climb up on to hurl snowballs. Once a wall is about two bricks high, build several vertical supports behind it from snow bricks carefully stacked on top of each other. Rest a board on top of the wall and the new supports. Now you have the perfect vantage point for hurling your snowballs. Just make sure it's stable before you climb on top.

Ice cream containers, plant pots, or buckets make great decorative snow bricks. So, when you've finished building your fort, why not add a layer of these bricks?

FORT WARNING

Check your fort regularly to make sure it is standing strong. You don't want it to fall down on you in the middle of a snowball battle.

Bad Spelling Bee

Anyone can learn to spell well, but it takes talent to get words wrong by spelling them as they sound. For example you could spell the word *potato* "poughteighteau." Here's where the sounds for this awful spelling come from:

Letter	Sound	Example
P	po	as in hippo
O	ough	as in though
T	t	as in take
A	eigh	as in neigh
T	t	as in take
O	eau	as in bureau

Or how about spelling the word *usage* "youzitch." This packs seven errors into a five-letter word. Can you beat that?

HOW TO PLAY

Dad challenges each player to come up with a word and devise the worst spelling he or she can for it. The players then have two minutes to come up with their final worst spelling and write it down.

Dad looks at each player's word and must be able to guess what the word is even though it is badly spelled. Players score one point for each wrong letter they managed to fit into the word.

Good words to start with are: Australia, diamond, fatigue, height, leopard, mayonnaise, mnemonic, rhinoceros, xylophone, and zucchini.

Have a Soccer Ball Juggling Contest

If you want to look like an international soccer star, you need to know how to juggle a soccer ball with your feet and body. This is also called the art of the keepie-uppie.

Stand on one leg with your other foot raised, the toes higher than the heel. Drop the ball onto the flat top of your foot as you flick your toes up lightly. You are trying to bounce the ball just an inch or two. The goal is to make sure the ball doesn't fly forward — if it does, you'll be lunging clumsily after it. Keep it bouncing up and spinning slightly back, toward your shin. You can even add a knee bounce now and then.

When you've mastered the keepie-uppie, have a contest to see who can do the most in one minute. Alternatively, face each other and do keepie-uppies until one person drops his or her ball.

EXPERT UPPIES

Try switching feet between kicks and letting the ball bounce off your chest. The ultimate art is to tip your head back and launch the ball up onto your forehead, balancing it there for a few seconds before letting it roll back down onto your foot.

Go on a Crab-fishing Expedition

In any coastal town or village where people have been crabbing for generations, local stores will sell lines and bags of bait.

However, if you need to make your own equipment, it's easy. Kite string makes a good fishing line, and if it comes with a plastic handle at one end, you'll have less trouble with tangling while you're angling.

The best time to catch a bucket full of crabs is when the tide is coming in. The perfect place to fish for them is from a pier at the mouth of an estuary, where a river meets the sea.

You will need:

• a crab line • a metal hook (the top of a wire coat hanger will work fine) • a metal weight • a large container • bait (baitfish or squid is good) • a fishing net

TAKE THE BAIT

Tie a piece of metal, such as a nut or bolt, near the end of your line to weigh it down.

 Tie a hook to the end of the line. It's there to hold your bait, not to catch your crustaceans, so it doesn't have to be sharp.

Bait the hook with a piece of fish about 2 inches by 2 inches. If the bait is too big, the crabs will be able to tear chunks off it. If it is too small, they won't be tempted to nibble at all. The crabs will grab the bait with their pincers, so don't worry, they won't get hurt by the hook.

Always wash your hands thoroughly after handling the bait.

Fill the container halfway with water and put it to one side. Then lower the baited line until it's on the estuary bed.

If you feel a gentle tug on your line, slowly pull up your line. Don't jerk it. If there is a crab on the line, get someone to hold a fishing net ready to scoop the crab up when it comes out of the water. Place the crab in your container, being careful of the pincers.

Repeat until you have a container full of crabs.

At the end of the expedition, carefully pour the crabs back into the water. Don't make them crabby by keeping them out of the water for too long.

Tip from Dad: Crabs prefer bait with a strong odor. The storekeeper will know which type of baitfish works best for crabbing.

CRABBY CONTESTS

Crabbing contests are great fun with everyone getting their own line, bait, and bucket.

First to Five: The first person to catch five crabs wins. The crabs must make it into the bucket. If they scuttle away or fall off the line, it doesn't count.

Biggest Crab Wins: Set a time limit. The person with the biggest specimen in his or her bucket at the end of that time is the winner.

Play Indoor Fishing

With this game, you can go on a fishing trip come rain or shine. Just don't try eating these flappy friends for dinner.

For two fishermen you will need:

• markers • sheets of white cardboard • scissors
• a plain, medium-size cardboard box • a box of
paper clips • 2 pieces of string, each at least 3 feet long
• 2 sticks • 2 magnets

To make a fishy template, draw a fish 6 inches long on a piece of cardboard. Cut it out. Then make as many fish as you want by placing the template on another sheet of cardboard, drawing around it and cutting out your catch.

 Have a competition to see who can decorate their fish the best, using the markers.

Now paint waves and seaweed around the outside of the box.

Write a number between five and ten on every fish. Then slide a paper clip over the nose of each one. Throw your fish into the box.

To make the fishing rods, tie lengths of string to the ends of the sticks, then tie a magnet to the end of each string.

See who can score the most points by dangling his or her magnet in the pond and taking turns to catch a fish by its paper clip.

Create a Cloud

Clouds are fascinating things. They may look light and fluffy, but they are actually made from minuscule water droplets. They can move at speeds of more than 100 miles per hour when the wind pushes them along.

Here's how to make a cloud in your kitchen using a clear plastic two-liter bottle, a match, and some water.

First, fill the bottle with hot water until it is about a third full. Put the top on the bottle and give it a good shake for a minute. As the water evaporates, water vapor will be produced in the air inside the bottle.

Unscrew the top of the bottle and hold a lit match just inside the opening for a few seconds. Drop the lit match into the bottle and immediately replace the cap. Watch as the space above the water fills with smoke and soot particles.

Give the bottle a tight squeeze then quickly release it. Keep squeezing and releasing the bottle until you see a cloud form.

Once you have created your cloud, take the cap off the bottle and watch your little cloud escape.

Tip from Dad: Make it easier to see the cloud by holding a sheet of black paper behind the bottle before squeezing.

THE SCIENCE BEHIND IT

In nature, a cloud is made when water vapor rises, experiences a drop in air pressure, cools, and then turns into tiny water droplets. This process is helped by solid particles, such as dust or smoke, being present in the air.

In the same way, the vapor inside the bottle cools when you stop squeezing it, because this creates a drop in air pressure. The smoke inside the bottle (solid particles) helps the vapor form tiny droplets and make a cloud.

Bust an Essential Surf Move

The first time you stand up on a surfboard and ride a breaking wave will be etched in your memory forever. As long as you can swim, you can learn to surf.

TAKE THE SKID TEST

Before you zip up your wet suit and climb on your board, you need to answer a very important question: Are you a "regular" or a "goofy"? If you did a running slide along a polished floor, would you lead with your left foot? If so, you are what surfers call regular-footed. If the right foot is out front you're goofy-footed. Neither is better than the other. It's all just a matter of instinct.

THE POP-UP

Here's how to master the essential surf move known as the pop-up. Practice it on dry land before you even think about testing your skills in the sea.

1. Lie facedown on the board. Your hands should be at your sides (shoulder-width apart), palms facing downward and level with your chest, as if about to do a push-up. Your legs should be touching.

2. Now, in one smooth movement, push up with your hands and straighten your arms.

3. In the same moment, pull your feet and knees under your body so you are crouching on the board, as shown above. Your butt should not be touching the board. Your leading foot (the one you discovered by sliding along the floor on page 24) should be slightly in front of the other.

4. Now come up into a standing position, with one foot in front of the other, knees bent. Your feet should be just more than shoulder-width apart. Your arms should be slightly bent and outstretched. Your back foot should be at a right angle to the board and the front foot at a slight diagonal. Keep your head held high and your eyes focused in front of you.

SURFBOARD SLANG

Now that you've learned how to stand like a surf dude, take turns testing each other's surf slang.

amped: hyper, overexcited
beached: stuffed full of food
gnarly: large or dangerous
rails: the surfboard's curved sides
stoked: happy, excited
wipe out: to fall off your board

Make an Artificial Eye

Why not make an artificial eye to look at the world? It's amazing what you can make with an empty cardboard tube!

You will need:

• a felt-tip pen or marker • a cardboard tube (the cylinder kind with a plastic lid that keeps round potato chips fresh — clean out any crumbs!) • a ruler • a craft knife • a thumbtack • a sheet of tracing paper • masking tape • aluminum foil

With a felt-tip pen or marker, draw a straight line around the tube about 2 inches from the closed base.

 Using a sharp craft knife, carefully cut the tube into two pieces along the line you have drawn.

With a thumbtack, poke a hole through the center of the metal base of the tube.

Cut a circle of tracing paper that fits snugly inside the plastic lid of the tube. This will act as the screen of your "eye." Secure it with some tape.

Put the plastic lid (with the screen inside) back onto the open end of the short piece of tube.

Next, put the long tube back on the other side of the lid, and tape it in place with masking tape.

To prevent light from leaking into the tube, roll it in a double layer of aluminum foil and tape the foil tightly into place.

You should now have something that looks a little bit like an aluminum foil telescope. This is your artificial eye.

On a bright sunny day, head outside and find an object that won't move, such as a tree or building. Hold the open end of your tube to one eye. Press it firmly against your face to cut out as much light as possible.

You should be able to see a color image that has been projected through the pinhole onto the screen. It will be an upside-down image.

Tip from Dad: If you can't see the image clearly, try putting a blanket over your head and poking the tube out of a gap in the material. This will reduce the amount of light that can leak into the end of the tube that is in front of your eye.

Take a Road Trip

Turn boring car journeys into road trips and you'll never hear "Are we there yet?" ever again. Here's how to make sure your four-wheeled adventure is one to remember.

DESTINATION UNKNOWN

Head for an interesting town or attraction you've never visited before, or decide on the general direction you want to head in and see where you end up. After all, the more spontaneous your trip, the greater the thrill.

Pack plenty of snacks and drinks to break up the journey. Nothing tastes better than root beer swigged straight from the bottle and homemade apple pie eaten with your fingers.

Make a road trip soundtrack: Each person brings five CDs for the open road so you can mix and match songs.

Don't be afraid to take a detour if something exciting crops up en route, such as a beautiful field or beach. Road trips are as much about the journey as the destination.

TIME FOR A CHAT

Why not take turns asking one another a question that you would never ask in normal life. Try "What was the best day of your life?" or "When are you happiest?"

For a bit of lighthearted chatter, try playing a game of "Never-ending Story." Take turns adding a sentence to a story that you make up on the spot, or give a popular fairy tale an amusing revamp. Even if you start somewhere obvious such as "Once upon a time, there were three bears," the story will soon take some unexpected twists: "'This is a stickup. Hand over your porridge!' shouted Goldilocks."

Learn a Capoeira Move

Question: Which sport combines martial arts and dance, and improves your balance and coordination?
Answer: Capoeira, a sport invented in the seventeenth century in Brazil.

If you want to impress your friends with some of the coolest moves on the planet, read on.

GINGA MOVE

The *ginga* is the most important move in capoeira. The word literally means "to rock back and forward" or to swing. This basic movement is a way of keeping the body prepared for other capoeira moves.

1. Stand with your feet shoulder-width apart. This will help you maintain your balance. Raise your left arm diagonally across your body and extend your left leg behind you.

2. Then, move your left leg forward again, taking a step sideways.

3. Next, raise your right arm and extend your right leg backward.

4. Take a step forward and to the right. Repeat this sequence.

Music is very important to capoeira, as it sets the tempo. Put on a CD. As you get into the rhythm of the move, it should start to "swing" and your limbs will feel free and easy.

Make a Glow-in-the-dark T-shirt

A glow-in-the-dark bat T-shirt is great for spooking your friends or neighbors on Halloween. Trick or treat!

You will need:

• a large potato • a vegetable knife • a pencil • paper
• scissors • cardboard • some newspaper • white and black
fabric paint • a plate • a black T-shirt • glow-in-the-dark
paint (available from a craft store) • a small paintbrush

 Cut the potato in half lengthwise using a vegetable knife.

 Practice drawing the outline of a bat on a piece of paper, then draw your final design on a piece of cardboard. Make sure your bat is no bigger than your potato half.

Cut out the cardboard bat to make a template. Place the bat on the potato and draw around it by scoring the potato with a pencil.

With the knife, cut away the potato surrounding the bat shape, so that the bat is left raised.

Fold a newspaper in half and tuck it inside the front of your T-shirt so it is behind the spot where you will print your bat.

Pour some white paint onto a plate, and dip your "bat-ato" into it. The surface of the bat should be covered with paint, but it should not be dripping.

Make a print on the front of the T-shirt by pressing the bat-ato firmly against the fabric. Do this once in the center of the shirt, or several times, so the front is covered with flapping bats. Wipe your bat-ato clean.

Leave the white paint to dry. Wash the plate, then pour glow-in-the-dark paint onto the plate.

Dip your bat-ato in the paint and press it on to the white bat on the T-shirt. The glow-in-the-dark paint will really stand out when printed over the white background. When the paint has dried, paint eyes and a mouth on your bat with black fabric paint.

When the bat has dried, put on your T-shirt and get ready to look scary.

Have a Plate-spinning Competition

Plate spinning will keep you occupied for hours. Always use plastic plates — that way you won't break anything and injure yourself in the process.

You will need:

- bamboo sticks
  (at least 3 feet long)
- plastic plates with a circular rim underneath
  (they need a slightly hollow underside
  that slopes in toward the center)

GOING SOLO

Start by holding a stick at a slight angle — imagine the angle an hour hand makes when it is pointing to two o'clock.

Pick up a plate and hang it from the stick by the rim.

Make a slow circular motion with your wrist, so that the plate starts to spin. Keep the rest of your arm still. Don't move your shoulder or elbow. Make sure the plate rolls around the stick, and doesn't get stuck on one spot. It should move like a spinning top, not a swinging lasso.

Gradually rotate the plate faster and faster until it levels out and is spinning horizontally. Then stop moving the stick. It should slide to the concave center of the plate, and for the next few seconds, the plate will spin by itself.

Don't panic if the plate starts to slow and wobble. Just give the stick a few more flicks with your wrist to keep it going.

THE TWO TIMER

Now that you've mastered the basic spin, switch the stick to your free hand by sliding your grip close to the plate, lifting your leg and handing the plate under your leg for extra effect. Then place another plate on the tip of a second stick, and spin the plates two-at-a-time. Be sure the plates don't collide with each other!

IN A SPIN

Kick off a contest to see who can spin a plate the longest. Then take your act outside and see who can spin the most plates at once. Push sticks into soft earth so you won't have to struggle to hold the plates as they spin.

As you set new plates spinning, give the other sticks a flick to keep them going.

If you manage to spin more than three plates at one time, congratulations — you should be in the circus!

COOL TRICKS

Lift the spinning plate off the stick with your index finger and hold it up high. Then flick it up in the air and catch it on the end of your finger.

Spin two plates, one in each hand. Throw both plates into the air at the same time and then catch them on the opposite sticks.

If you're feeling really bold, why not make the plate spin really quickly, tip your head back, and balance the end of the stick on your chin? Remember: Practice makes perfect.

Hold a Garage Sale

A garage sale is a fun way to get rid of unwanted household clutter and turn it into cash that can help fund a road trip, a crab-fishing expedition, or perhaps your favorite charity.

Before you start searching for moneymakers, read the following tips.

IT'S A DATE

A good garage sale needs a lot of planning. Your customers won't just appear by magic — you have to give them plenty of warning about your bargain bonanza.

Start by setting a date and time for the sale as far in advance as possible – at least one month.

Pick a Saturday or Sunday if you can. Make sure your sale doesn't clash with holidays and other events in the area, such as parades and parties.

READ ALL ABOUT IT

 Make some colorful posters advertising the date, time, and place of your sale.

Put up your posters around your neighborhood. Try giving some flyers to friends and neighbors. Work as a team to advertise your sale.

WHAT TO SELL

Search your house thoroughly for any unwanted items that you could sell.

Join forces to look in rooms, closets, and under beds. Don't forget to peer into the depths of the garage and attic if you have them.

If you're not sure whether to sell something, apply this basic rule: If you've forgotten you had it, you definitely won't miss it. Just don't sell anything that isn't yours without the owner's permission!

Books, CDs, toys, and kitchen utensils tend to sell easily, but don't be afraid to put every bit of junk you can find on the sales table. It might look useless to you, but it could make somebody else's day.

Clothes will sell best if you display them on a clothes rack. Cups and dishes will be purchased quickly if you box them up in sets. It's easier to get rid of items such as paperbacks and CDs if you price them individually.

A long table is perfect for displaying your wares.

If you're selling electrical items, such as power drills and blenders, make sure they are in safe working order first. Keep an extension cord handy to show customers that the items work properly.

Be prepared to sit outside all day in order to maximize your profit, and make sure young vendors are supervised at all times.

THE PRICE IS RIGHT

Don't price too high. Be prepared to haggle with customers and always sell at a low price if the alternative is no sale at all. After all, if you didn't want to sell it, what's it doing on the table?

Tags and stickers can turn off buyers, but if something is a real bargain, why not display its price?

Tip from Dad: To get your sale noticed and have some extra fun, why not give your sale a theme? If it's Halloween, dress up in scary costumes and offer free spider juice (apple juice with green food coloring) to the first ten customers.

Hold a Stone-skipping Contest

All you need to hold a stone-skipping contest is some flat stones and some water, of course. The stones should not be so light that they flip over, or so heavy that you won't be able to throw them properly. Oval-shaped stones work best.

THE TECHNIQUE

Cup the stone with your thumb and index finger so that you make a C-shape. Your other fingers should be curved underneath the stone.

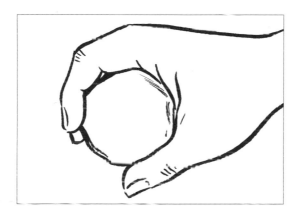

Stand with your legs apart and your knees bent, with one foot leading. If you are holding the stone in your right hand, step forward on your left leg and vice versa.

As you sweep your arm back, try to keep the stone as low and flat as possible (ideally you want the stone to stay nearly parallel to the surface of the water — at an angle of no more than 10 or 20 degrees).

Then jerk the stone forward, using plenty of spin in your wrist and index finger.

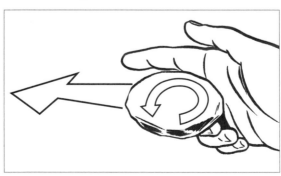

If the stone hits the water front-edge first, it will disappear like a diving duck. If you can, angle the stone so it's almost flat, but with its nose pointing upward a fraction. This way it is more likely to bounce right across the pond.

WHY THE BOUNCE?

The stone bounces because the surface tension of the water acts like a trampoline. As the stone pushes down, the water pushes upward.

Did you know?
The world stone-skipping record is held by Russell Byars, called Rock Bottom by his friends, from Pittsburgh, Pennsylvania. He made a stone skip fifty-one times in a single throw.

Put Your Bedroom Underwater

Turn a boring bedroom into an underwater paradise by creating an underwater mural. Instead of waking up in your bedroom, you'll wake to find yourself beneath the Caribbean Sea.

TRANSFORMATION

Using a piece of chalk, draw two horizontal lines that divide your wall from floor to ceiling into three roughly equal bands. Paint the top band (the one nearest the ceiling) sky blue.

When the paint is dry, use your chalk to draw wave crests along the line at the top of your middle band. If the waves come out wrong, you can wash off the chalk and start again.

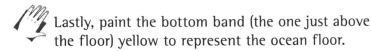 Using a darker blue than you used for the sky, paint the middle band on your wall, filling in the crests of your waves, too.

Lastly, paint the bottom band (the one just above the floor) yellow to represent the ocean floor.

Now you can start filling the scene with fish. In no time at all, you will be surrounded by sharks, electric eels, jellyfish, and octopuses. Practice them on paper, then sketch your sea creatures on the wall with chalk before filling them in with different colored paint. Paint in plenty of colorful coral and tropical fish, too, as well as seaweed and anemones.

Add some pebbles and shells to the seabed. How about some starfish, lobsters, and sea urchins with deadly spines that help fend off unwanted visitors?

Make a Tiny Parachute

Make a toy parachute and watch it float to earth. All you need is a circle of cotton fabric 12 inches in diameter and eight pieces of thick thread each about 14 inches long.

Pinch the fabric at a point along the edge of the circle. Tie the end of a length of thread around the gather and knot the string. Tie the dangling end to a small, lightweight toy, such as a plastic soldier. Repeat this for each piece of thread at regular intervals around the fabric.

Outside, or in a large indoor space, pinch the center of the fabric circle and pull it into a thin cone. Swing the toy around, then let go, sending it high into the air. As the toy falls, the parachute will open.

Experiment to discover the lowest height that allows the chute to open successfully. Does it work from the bottom of the stairs or when you stand on a chair?

Why not make a parachute for each member of your family and see whose stays in the air longest?

Send a Mysterious Message in a Bottle

Eye-catching decoration is the key to successful bottle-mail. Few people will pick up an ugly-looking bottle, but if it is colorfully decorated, no one will be able to resist. Choose a glass bottle with a tight-fitting cork. Why not use enamel paints to create a desert island scene with yellow sand and green palm trees? Alternatively, why not paint "Open Me!" in multicolored letters?

THE MESSAGE

Make the message that goes inside your bottle as imaginative and intriguing as possible, so that the finder replies. Write it as a series of clues describing where the bottle has come from or try composing a poem:

> *This bottle it did travel*
> *From far-off distant lands,*
> *Until this bottle landed*
> *In a stranger's hands.*
> *The owners of this bottle*
> *Would be so very glad*
> *To hear that you have found it,*
> *What a journey it has had!*

Use good quality writing paper that won't be destroyed when the bottle is tossed from side to side in the water.

Don't forget to include some contact details, such as an e-mail address, on the back of your message. Never write your telephone number or street address on the message, though — there is no need to give out such personal information.

IT'S A SEAL

The cork has to be a perfect fit for your bottle. Even a single drop of water could damage your message.

Once corked, seal the bottle by lighting a candle and dripping a thin layer of wax around the cork.

THERE SHE GOES

You want your bottle to travel as far as possible, so ideally, choose a launch point near the open sea. Don't throw the bottle into a bay or a harbor — it won't get very far. If you are throwing the bottle into a stream, make sure it is at a point where the river is deep so the bottle won't smash on the riverbed or stones.

The best time to launch your bottle is just after high tide, when the currents are running fast. Throw the bottle as far as possible from the shore or riverbank. Cross your fingers and wait patiently. There's no way to know where your little vessel will end up, or who will find it.

Warning: Make sure you are not breaking any local littering laws before you send your message in a bottle.

Did you know?
Opening a message in a bottle could get you killed in Elizabethan England. Only the royal Uncorker of Ocean Bottles was allowed to open such bottles, as they often contained messages from spies.

Have a Finger Soccer Match

You don't need a park and two teams of people to play a lively game of soccer. A kitchen table, a Ping-Pong ball, and your fingers will do just fine.

Use a piece of chalk to mark out your field on a large, flat surface.

Place two open cardboard boxes on their sides to be your goals.

Use your index finger and middle finger to "run" across the table and to dribble the ball. You could make boots like the ones shown above with cardboard and papier-mâché, but bare fingers work just as well.

Make sure each team has an equal number of players. Two players can have an excellent match and can play using their left and right hands — one hand playing an attack position, the other staying in defense. This takes practice and it helps if the field isn't too large.

THE RULES

• Keep one of your fingers in contact with the ground at all times. Superhuman leaps and "flying" players are not allowed.

• Take a kick-off from the middle of the table after every goal.

• Corners and penalties are handled in the same way as in a full-size game. If you grab your opponent's fingers, or push or hold them away from the ball, that's a foul and your opponent gets a free kick.

• Your opponent gets a penalty kick if a foul occurs in the goal area.

• Five fouls add up to a yellow card, and two yellow cards mean a red card. A red card means a player can only use one hand.

• Holding the ball between your fingers or cupping the ball under your palm and using your thumb are both finger soccer offenses. Putting one finger on the ball to hold it in place before kicking it away is, however, fair play.

Create a Magical Work of Art

It's time for Dad to use his artistic talents for fun, instead of just painting the living room ceiling. Here's how to create a mesmerizing picture using crayons and black paint.

You will need:

• a multicolored pack of crayons • sheets of thick paper that won't tear easily — the bigger the better • newspaper • an old fork • black poster paint • a 4-inch-wide paintbrush

Using different colored crayons, decorate a sheet of paper with swirling patterns. Fill every inch with whirls and squiggles. Press down hard, and go back over your design. Take a long, loving look at your stunning masterpiece before you cover it up.

Put the sheet on a newspaper and brush black poster paint over it. Coat it generously, so there isn't a trace of color left.

Now leave the paint to dry.

Test the paint with your fingertip — the effect will be ruined if you start working when it is still wet.

When you are sure the paint is dry, take the fork and scrape its prongs against the black paint to create one of these spectacular pieces of art:

- magical tigers at midnight

- jewels in an underground cavern

- planets in a distant galaxy

- explorers in their rainbow space rockets

- parrots in the deepest jungle (use dark green poster paint instead of black)

Have Some Egg-cellent Fun

Eggs are much tougher than you think. To prove it, stand over the kitchen sink, and roll up your sleeves. Put an egg in the palm of your hand and close your fingers around it. Try to crush the egg without using your thumb. It's nearly impossible — even for Dad.

A TALL ORDER

You can drop an egg from a height without breaking it — you just need to make sure it lands on grass.

The trick is to make sure the egg lands at an angle, pointed end down, and that it's moving forward at about the same speed as it is falling.

A good way to prove this — if you have a large yard or you can get to a park — is to throw an egg as far and as high as you can. As it lands, it should be traveling forward as well as down and won't smash, unless of course it hits a tree on its way! Make sure you clean up any eggy mess.

RECORD BREAKING

The world record for dropping an egg from a height without it breaking is held by David Donoghue. In 1994, he threw an ordinary egg out of a helicopter 700 feet above a golf course and retrieved it whole.

PLAY EGG CATCH

To play egg catch, everyone needs an apron or an old raincoat worn backward.

Find an open, grassy area. Stand three steps from your opponent, and start playing catch with an egg. After two throws, each player takes a step back. Repeat this until you have thrown the egg twenty times. Now you'll be quite far apart, and it will get more and more difficult. The loser is the person who drops or fails to catch the egg and causes it to break.

If you have four or more players, pair off. Each pair should stand opposite each other and throw an egg from one player to the other. After each successful catch, both players take a large step back and throw again. See who can make the longest throw without smashing the egg or getting egg on their opponent's face! You're unlikely to beat the world record set by Keith Thomas and Johnie Dell Foley in 1978 of 323 feet and 2 inches.

YUMMY SCRAMBLED EGGS

If you've still got a few eggs in one piece after the game, why not whip up some delicious scrambled eggs?

For two people you will need:

- 6 eggs • 5 tablespoons milk • 1 tablespoon butter
  - salt and pepper to taste

Whisk the eggs in a large bowl, then add the milk, salt, and pepper. Beat them all together.

 Heat a large nonstick saucepan over medium heat.

Melt the butter in the saucepan, then add the egg mix.

Turn the heat to low. Once the eggs begin to cook, start scrambling them by moving them back and forth with a wooden spoon to break them up.

Keep scrambling until the eggs are cooked. Then turn off the heat and serve immediately with toast.

A Puzzling Pavement Trick

To see just how low some people will stoop, try this sneaky coin trick.

 Superglue a length of transparent nylon thread to a coin. Be careful not to superglue a finger to the coin in the process. Leave the glue to dry.

Now choose a busy outdoor spot, such as a park or a shopping center. Find a place where you can position the coin so people will see it, but where you can hide nearby and not be seen.

Hold on to the other end of the thread, making sure the line stays taut. Wait until someone passing by bends to pick up the coin, then quickly tug the coin toward you and away from one very confused passerby.

Beat the Buzzer

The goal of this game is to guide a wire loop along a length of zigzagging metal without the loop and metal touching.

You will need:

- a wire coat hanger • a piece of flat wood approximately 8 inches by 4 inches • an electric doorbell buzzer
- a screwdriver • a 3-volt battery • rubber-coated flexible wire • a drinking straw • screws • insulating tape
- a pair of pliers • wire cutters • a drill

Snip the hook off the hanger and open it up. Twist the wire into a series of curves leaving a straight section at each end. Using pliers, bend each end into a tiny C-shape.

Drill a small hole in the wooden base near each end. Put the tip of a screw through each C-shape and screw the wire onto the wood.

Tape a 3-volt battery to the base. Cut a short length of flexible wire and strip back the rubber insulation at both ends. Tape one end to the negative terminal of the battery and wrap the other end around one of the buzzer's electrical terminals.

Cut another short length of flexible wire and strip back the rubber insulation on both ends. Wrap one

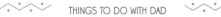
end around the buzzer's other terminal and the other end around the screw at one end of the metal wire.

Slide a drinking straw onto another length of flexible wire and strip back 4 inches of the rubber insulation from one end. Bend this into an O-shape loop around your zigzagging metal wire. Then twist the loop shut without squashing it.

Strip the other end of the flexible wire and connect it to the positive terminal of the battery. If the loop touches the wiggly wire, it will complete the electrical circuit and set off the buzzer.

IT'S A BUZZ

Take turns holding the straw and guide the loop along the wire without touching it and setting off the buzzer. The winner is the person who gets the furthest along without the buzzer sounding.

Tip from Dad: When you've finished playing, disconnect one of the wires and tape it to the wood so you don't drain the battery.

Make a Thread-spool Snake

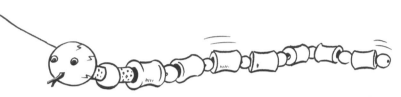

This toy snake slithers like a real snake, but the good news is it won't ever bite.

You will need:

• a large darning needle and thick thread • 7 empty thread spools • a string of large beads • a hammer and nail • two corks • a Ping-Pong ball • a small piece of felt • glue • paints

Thread the darning needle and tie a knot at one end. Feed the needle through one of the beads, then through an empty thread spool.

Keep threading a bead and then a spool onto the thread until all the spools have been used.

 Make a hole in each of the corks by carefully hammering a nail into it lengthwise then removing the nail. Now add a cork, a bead, and another cork to the snake.

Use the needle to make two holes on either side of the Ping-Pong ball. Run the needle through the Ping-Pong ball to make the snake's head. Then tie off the thread.

Cut out an inch-long piece of felt, then snip one end into a V-shape. This is the snake's forked tongue. Glue the tongue to the head.

 Paint eyes and zigzag markings on the ball. Then decorate the spools in snakelike colors.

Tie a piece of string around the neck of the snake.

Once it has dried, grab hold of your snake and watch it slither.

Have a Thumb-wrestling Contest

Thumb wrestling might be one of the world's smallest sports, but it requires a lot of energy and concentration. In this frantic game, lock hands with an opponent and try to pin down his or her thumb without your own thumb getting trapped. The winner is the person who pins down his or her opponent's thumb the greatest number of times in one game.

RULE OF THUMB

• Before the match starts, agree on the number of rounds that will be played. Each round ends when a thumb is pinned down by another thumb for at least four seconds.

• Decide whether index fingers are allowed to wrestle as well as thumbs. It is easier if your index finger "snakes" around your opponent's top knuckle to help hold his or her wriggly thumb, so if you want to keep fingers out of the match, agree on the following pledge:

No snakes, no buddies, and no tag teams.

This means neither contestant is allowed to move any fingers, just his or her thumb.

• Remember, this isn't an arm-wrestling competition. Your elbows and wrists must not move.

IN THE RING

To make a professional-looking thumb-wrestling ring you will need a piece of sturdy cardboard or light wood.

 Cut two holes for the thumbs about 2 inches apart. If using wood, smooth the edges of the holes with sandpaper to avoid painful splinters.

LET THE GAME BEGIN

Make sure both players understand and agree on the rules in advance so there is less chance of an argument developing.

Sit down at a table with your chair facing your opponent.

Both players must wrestle using the same hand — right hand to right hand, or left hand to left hand.

Bend the chosen hand to make a curved C-shape without any gaps between your fingers. Keeping your hand in this position, link C's with your opponent, with the underside of your fingers touching.

Press the tips of your thumbs together and start the game by chanting a rhyme such as:

One, two, three, four, I declare a thumb war!
Five, six, seven, eight, try to keep your thumb straight.

Throughout the chant, each contestant repeatedly moves his or her thumb to either side of his or her opponent's thumb. As soon as the chant has ended, the match begins.

Wriggle, bend, and twist your thumb to grab the other player's thumb and pin it down for a count of four, chanting, "One, two, three, four, 1 won the thumb war!"

Repeat until an agreed-upon number of rounds have been played, or until someone is scared he or she might dislocate his or her thumb!

If all else fails, do your best to distract your opponent by making him or her laugh or lose his or her concentration. It's totally fair and part of the fun of thumb wrestling.

Tip from Dad: Why not give each thumb a bandanna by tying a tiny strip of colored material around its top.

Create a Campfire Classic

You don't have to go far to enjoy a night under the stars. Why not set up camp right in your backyard? What is essential, however, is the classic campfire treat — s'mores.

To prepare s'mores, you'll need a campfire, but if you don't want a charred mess in the middle of your lawn, you can use a charcoal barbecue grill.

SUPER S'MORES

You will need:

- a package of graham crackers • a large bar of chocolate
- a bag of marshmallows • some metal skewers

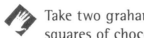 Start by making sure your campfire or your barbecue is ready. When preparing s'mores, it's best to have a fire that is glowing rather than flaming.

Take two graham crackers and add a couple of squares of chocolate to one of them.

Slide two marshmallows on a skewer and hold them just above the flames of the campfire. Keep heating them until the marshmallows are golden brown and deliciously soft. The skewers might get very hot, so make sure you hold them at the end.

Warning: Make sure your marshmallows don't catch fire. If they do, quickly blow them out before they melt and fall off the skewer.

With the marshmallows still on the skewer, place them on top of the chocolate on the graham cracker. Then take the other graham cracker and make a sandwich. Squeeze them together as you pull out the skewer, leaving the marshmallows between the graham crackers.

Wait until the marshmallows are cool enough to eat before you dig in.

Delicious. Pass some more s'mores, please!

Make a Scarecrow

If you are throwing a party and you want to give it a quirky twist, why not make a scarecrow to welcome your guests? With a sign around his neck and a hand pointing to the fun, he'll bring an instant grin to their faces.

You will need:

- a bamboo pole that is 9 feet long • old clothes
- newspaper or straw (or another type of stuffing)
- a pillowcase • a marker
- string • glue • 2 buttons • rubber bands
- a pair of gloves • a sheet of card stock

Cut the pole into two pieces, one 3 feet long and the other 6 feet long. Tie the short pole about 20 inches from the end of the long pole to make a cross.

Put a shirt on your scarecrow, using the short pole as his arms, and button it. Knot it at the waist. Stuff the shirt with scrunched up newspaper or anything else that's handy, such as dry leaves. Fill the arms as well as the torso.

Put a jacket over the shirt if you want your scarecrow to look really dapper.

Pull a pair of gloves over the ends of the arms and secure them with rubber bands. Make sure the tip of the pole fits

into an index finger of one glove so that your scarecrow can point the way to the party.

Pull one leg of a pair of pants onto the main pole and up around the stuffed shirt. Use string to tie the pants securely around the scarecrow's waist, so they stay in place.

Stuff both legs with more newspaper before tying string around the bottom of each leg to keep the stuffing in.

Draw a face on a pillowcase with the marker. Glue or sew on two buttons for eyes.

Fill the pillowcase with newspaper and tie it onto the pole before adding a hat, scarf, and any other items you like.

Now write a welcome message in bright letters on a sheet of card stock. Tie the card stock around your scarecrow's neck then stand him by the door or plant him in the garden.

SPOOKY SCARECROW

 If you are making your scarecrow to welcome guests to a Halloween party, why not make the head from a pumpkin? Slice off the bottom of the pumpkin and hollow out the insides. Cut out two triangular eyes (with the points facing down), a triangle for the nose, and carve a jagged, toothy grin.

Mount your pumpkin head on the pole.

Warning: Do not put a lit candle anywhere near your scarecrow   particularly not in its pumpkin head. Anything made from newspaper or straw will catch fire before you can say "spooky."

Learn the Swimmer's Turn

A flip turn is a fantastic way to speed up your swimming and is guaranteed to make you look really cool. Moreover, in a family race, this stylish somersault is a great way for younger swimmers to gain a few yards on Dad.

Warning: Practice these somersaults in the middle of the pool, far away from the sides, until you have mastered them. You don't want to bang your head mid-turn.

NOW IT'S YOUR TURN

1. Swim toward the wall of the pool — keep an eye out for it, because you really don't want to head-butt the tiles! (You might want to wear goggles when practicing your somersault so that you are able see the wall more clearly.)

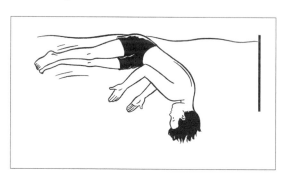

2. When you are an arm's length away from the wall, begin your somersault. Tuck your chin into your chest and scoop your arms toward your feet to propel yourself into the turn.

3. Bend your body forward at the waist. Position your hands on either side of your head, with your elbows tucked in. Roll your body into a ball and continue the somersault.

4. Halfway through (when your head is parallel to the floor of the pool again), start to uncurl your body. Straighten your arms, pointing your hands, back toward the center of the pool. Kick your legs out toward the wall and plant both of your feet firmly against it. Be careful not to kick the wall, as it will hurt!

5. Using both feet, push off from the wall and propel your body forward through the water. At the same time, rotate your body so that you are no longer on your back, but are on your front, belly down.

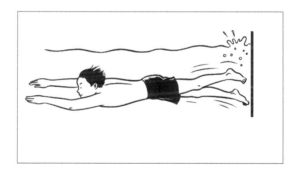

6. Stretch your arms in front of your head and streamline your body like a torpedo. Kick your legs underwater to drive yourself forward and swim up to the surface of the water to take a breath.

Start swimming strongly toward the opposite end of the pool. The last one there loses!

Make a Canine Cake

It's easy to forget that dogs have birthdays, too. Pets don't want video games or DVDs. What matters most to the average mutt is a tasty treat.

Why not make a meaty "birthday bone" cake from a can of dog food? You don't even need to use an oven.

Empty a medium-size can of chunky, meaty dog food onto an old baking sheet.

Divide the contents in two, and mold one half into a flat bar about 6 inches long. If you don't want to touch the meat with your fingers, wear clean rubber gloves.

Break the other half into four pieces and roll them into balls. Flatten these with the palm of your hand, and place two at each end of the "bone," smoothing out the joints as much as possible.

Open a can of tuna, drain away the oil or water, and sprinkle it over your dog-food bone as fishy "icing."

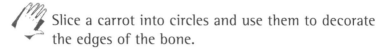 Slice a carrot into circles and use them to decorate the edges of the bone.

Warning: Chocolate is poisonous to dogs, so don't be tempted to add any to a canine's cake.

Add some candles on your canine cake and light them. Just make sure someone blows the candles out before your pet starts eating. You don't want to burn any noses.

If you don't have a dog of your own, make a cake for one of your relative's dogs or for a neighbor's helpful hound.

CAT CAKE

It is really easy to make a birthday cake for a cat, too. Just mold a small can of cat food into a semicircle. To make it look like a mouse, add a circle of carrot for an ear, and raisins to make an eye and a nose. For a real treat, add a trail of cream for a tail. That really is the cat's meow!

Invent a Secret Handshake

Everyone knows the importance of a firm handshake. Instead of a limp grasp of the fingers, aim for a confident grip and a smile. Secret handshakes are much cooler and can involve elbows, shoulders, and even feet.

Try these moves, then put some together in a cool combination to make your own family handshake.

- Hook your fingertips together.

- Raise your hands so they are facing the other person and slap each other's palms in a "high ten."

- Hold out both hands, palms facing up to be slapped.

- Wrap both hands around the other person's fist.

- Bump opposite elbows with each other twice.

- Bump opposite shoulders with each other three times.

- Hold your hands together, as if you're praying, then touch your middle fingers to your friend's middle fingers.

- Take turns lightly slapping the back of the other person's right hand.

- Link arms and hop around in a circle.

- Jump toward each other and bounce your chests together. (Don't attempt this if Dad has a big belly!)

SHAKE HANDS STREET STYLE

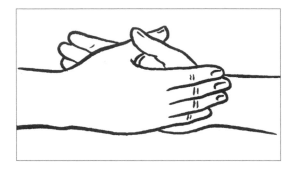

1. Start with an ordinary handshake.

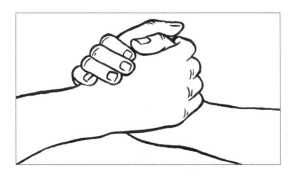

2. Drop your wrist so that your hands twist to a 90-degree angle and hook your thumbs together.

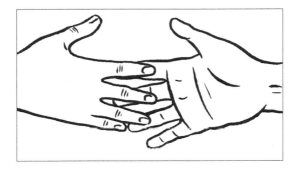

3. Slide your hands apart, wiggling your fingers to tickle each other's palm.

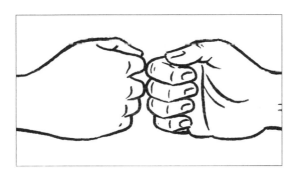

4. Bunch your hand into a fist and tap the top of the other person's fist twice. Let their fist bounce twice on yours. Then lightly punch your knuckles together.

Build a Water Obstacle Course

You'll need steady hands and balance to race around an obstacle course carrying a full cup of water.

This is an outdoor game, unless you want to turn your living room into a swimming pool. You don't need a big space to play it, just a big imagination.

HOW TO PLAY

The race starts at a small kiddie pool full of water, or a faucet, and ends with a row of buckets, one for each player.

Each contestant holds a plastic cup of water and races around an obstacle course before emptying the water into the bucket. This is repeated ten times. The winner is the player with the most water in his or her bucket at the end.

To avoid any confusion over whose bucket is whose, label each one with a contestant's name.

THE OBSTACLES

Hunt around your home and yard for objects that can be turned into obstacles. Try some of these challenges and experiment by building your own obstacles and inventing your own moves. (Don't forget to take a cup of water with you.)

- Walk backward around the kiddie pool.

- Run around a lawn chair three times.

- Walk along a plank balanced on bricks.

- Hop back and forth over a bamboo cane four times.

- Do three keepie-uppies with a soccer ball (see page 16).

- If you are feeling brave and don't mind getting drenched, balance the cup on your head for three seconds.

Tip from Dad: Make the challenge even harder by not allowing racers to cover their cups with their hands.

To even up the challenge, give younger players bigger cups or saucepans. Or instead of buckets, give them ice cream tubs to fill at the end.

Make a Feather Quill

Write the way your ancestors did with a handmade feather-quill pen.

You will need:

- a feather about 12 inches long (a turkey or goose feather from your local craft store or an online craft store works best)
- a can filled with sand
- a craft knife • a bottle of ink

It is a good idea to get Dad to do the hot and sharp parts of this project. He can create a tailor-made quill pen for each member of the family.

Carefully trim strands or "tines" of the feather away from the stem until you can hold the stem without being tickled. Medieval scribes would cut all the tines off, but it looks much nicer if some are left at the end.

To make the stem strong, place a can full of sand in an oven at 350°F for 20 minutes.

Using oven mitts, remove the (very hot) can and place it on a heatproof surface.

Push the tip of the feather deep into the sand and leave it there until the sand cools.

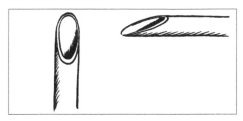

Ask the person whose pen it will be to hold the quill and check the position he or she feels most comfortable gripping it (usually people like to hold the stem's curve up against their index finger). Then use the knife to slice the end away, on the underside, by making a half-inch cut at a shallow angle.

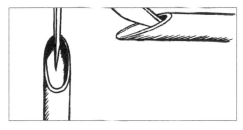

With the point of the knife, split the tip along the middle for 3/4 inch.

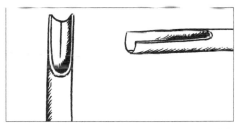

Cut the tip to make it into a crescent shape, like the letter C. This is the trickiest part.

Now shape the nib by making a curving cut on either side of the split, to make a sharp tip. Be careful not to cut the nib into too sharp a point.

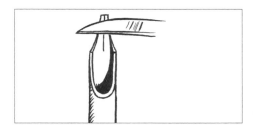

Use the flat part of the knife blade to scrape the inside of the tip clean. If the stem is thick, you might want to sharpen the nib from the inside with a tiny cut.

Now it's time to try out your quill. Dip the nib into a bottle of ink and get writing. It's trickier than using a ballpoint pen, but your letters will look really great with a little practice.

Tip from Dad: After about 1,000 words, you'll find the nib gets blunt. Just slice the tip of the quill off to make another nib.

Make a Treasure Map

Why not make an ancient treasure map of your backyard? Bury some treasure where X marks the spot. Then see if the rest of the family can follow the map.

To make paper look like an ancient sheet of parchment, all you need to do is soak it in cold, strong black tea for about five minutes.

Remove the paper from the tea and spread it out on a baking sheet.

Turn the oven on to its lowest setting (200°F). Place the baking sheet in the bottom of the oven until the corners of the paper start to curl. Then carefully remove the tray from the oven using oven mitts.

Warning: When it is in the oven, Dad should keep a close eye on the map.

For a really authentic effect, use a quill (see pages 80 to 82) to draw your map on the paper. Alternatively, draw your map in pen.

Add some islands and ships and draw an *x* to mark where the treasure is hidden.

Shiver me timbers — it's a real treasure map!

Catch a Shadow

Believe it or not, it really *is* possible to catch someone's shadow. Here's how.

You will need:

- poster putty • large sheets of white paper • a flashlight
- a pencil • black paper • a glue stick • tape • scissors

Use the poster putty to attach a large piece of white paper to a wall. Have one person stand sideways next to the wall about 2 feet away from the paper. This person is the "sitter" whose shadow will be caught.

Draw the curtains closed to darken the room and shine the flashlight onto the sitter's profile. Experiment with the distance between the light and the sitter until you get a sharp shadow of his or her profile that fits on the sheet of paper. The closer you move the flashlight to the sitter, the larger the shadow or silhouette will be.

Draw around the outline of the silhouette with a pencil. Then take down the paper and cut out the profile.

Tape the paper profile to a sheet of black paper. Using the white cutout as a template, snip around it again so that the profile is cut out in black paper.

Finally, use the glue stick to mount the black cutout onto a new sheet of white paper. Write your sitter's name and the date at the bottom of the paper.

FREESTYLE SILHOUETTE

In Victorian times, there was a craze for pictures like these. People became skilled at cutting tiny portraits out of paper without even drawing them first. Why not try cutting a profile of each other's faces from a black sheet of paper without drawing the outline? It's more tricky than it sounds.

Did you know?
The silhouette was named after French politician Etienne de Silhouette, who died in 1767. He was a mean, tightfisted man, and people joked he wouldn't waste his money on a painted portrait when he could have a paper cutout instead.

Create Your Own Fantastic Fossils

Create your very own dinosaur and footprint fossils.

You will need:

- a small cup full of cold coffee grounds • 2 cups of flour
- 6 tablespoons of salt • 3/4 cup of cold water • a sheet of waxed paper • a baking sheet • a plastic dinosaur (shells, twigs, and leaves make great fossils, too)

Put the cold coffee grounds, flour, salt, and water in a bowl and mix together to make a dough. The dough should not be so soft that it sticks to your fingers. If this is the case, add more flour.

Put the waxed paper on the baking sheet. Break the dough into small balls and place them on top of the paper. Squash the balls into disks with the palm of your hand.

Turn the toy dinosaur sideways and press it into each disk of dough. Then carefully peel it out to leave perfect dino-imprints.

 Bake the fossils on low heat until they are hard. When they come out they will look delicious, but don't be tempted to eat them!

FOOTPRINT FOSSILS

You will need:

• modeling clay • waxed paper • a hard-boiled egg (in its shell) • a pencil • plaster of paris • water

Knead the clay and roll it out into a thick, flat disk on a sheet of waxed paper. Make a raised rim around the edge of the disk by pressing a long sausage-shaped piece of clay around the rim.

Press the bottom of the egg into the clay — then lift it out. The imprint made is the middle of the dinosaur's foot. With your finger make four toe imprints around the foot.

Use a pencil to scratch out a vicious claw at each toe tip.

Mix a cup of plaster of paris in a bowl with 1/2 cup of water, and stir it into a soupy paste. Pour the paste into the hollow footprint, making sure there are no air bubbles. Leave to set, then peel the clay away from your footprint.

Harness Balloon Power

Does Dad have enough patience to make a jet-powered toy using a party balloon?

MAKE A MINI JET BOAT

Who needs a real-life speedboat when you can create a miniature version to race in your bathtub?

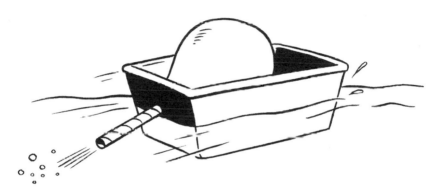

You will need:

• a lump of modeling clay • a large, wide, flat plastic container • a balloon • scissors • the barrel of a ballpoint pen • a rubber band

Start by placing a lump of modeling clay in one end of the plastic container. This will ensure the boat sits deep in the water instead of bobbing on top.

With the scissors, pierce the end of the container (the one that is closest to the lump of clay) near the base. Make a hole just big enough to poke the plastic pen barrel through.

Slip the pen barrel through the hole you made in the container and into the neck of the balloon. Seal the hole around the pen with more modeling clay. The balloon will be resting inside your container. Secure it by wrapping the rubber band tightly around the end.

Blow through the pen barrel to inflate the balloon. This takes a lot of air! When you are finished blowing, hold your finger over the hole at the end of the barrel to keep the air from escaping.

Now put the speedboat in a bathtub or small pool and remove your thumb from the hole to watch it go!

Tip from Dad: Why not each make a boat and see whose boat sails for the longest amount of time? You could even try racing them.

How to Play Achi

This game, which originated in West Africa, is ideal for two people to enjoy. It can be played almost anywhere, but is particularly perfect to play at the beach.

In the sand, mark out the lines of the square board as shown below. Hunt for a collection of pebbles and shells to use as counters — you'll need four of each.

HOW TO PLAY

One person plays using pebbles, the other with shells.

Toss a coin to decide which player starts. Then, taking turns, place your counters on the "board" at any of the points where lines intersect. When all eight counters are in position, players take turns moving their counters into the single empty spot, aiming to be the first player to get three counters in a row.

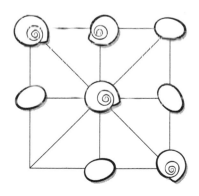

Make a Rain Stick

A rain stick is a South American musical instrument made from a cactus filled with hundreds of seeds and small stones. When the stick is turned upside down the seeds and stones make a sound like raindrops falling on leaves. Native South Americans believe this sound encourages the gods to make it rain. Here's how to make a rain stick without a cactus.

You will need:

• cardboard tubes, the sturdier the better
• carpet tacks with flat heads • seeds, beads, dry lentils, or even pieces of gravel • cardboard • tape • shells and straws to decorate your rain stick • paints

Tape your tubes together to make a long, hollow "stick."

Push or hammer carpet tacks into your stick in a spiral pattern stretching from one end of the tube to the other. The more tacks you use, the noisier your rain stick will be, but make sure that the points of the tacks don't poke through the other side of the tube.

Cut a circle of cardboard, and tape it over one end of the stick to seal it. Now pour in handfuls of seeds, lentils, gravel, and beads. Seal the other end with another circle of cardboard to make sure the contents will not fall out all over the floor.

Paint your rain stick with bright tropical colors. Why not add shell patterns and some feathers cut from colored paper?

For the best effect, don't shake the rain stick. Simply turn it on one end and let the contents trickle through the spikes. Then turn it over again, like an egg timer. Then wait and see if it rains!

Get "Tuned In"

"Tuned In" is a game that costs absolutely nothing to play. All you need is a radio, a timer or stopwatch, and some paper and pens.

HOW TO PLAY

Each player takes turns tuning the radio to a random station and leaving it there for 10 seconds. That player scores points depending on what is being broadcast on the station he or she has selected. The winner is the person who scores the most points in one hour.

Tip from Dad: You might also like to keep a blindfold handy to keep players from peeking at the frequency of the radio as they turn the dial or change the station.

This table shows the points awarded for each thing you might hear over the radio. If there is an overlap during those 10 seconds, the first thing heard counts.

• Music: 1 point
Bonus: An extra 3 points if you can name the song or piece of music, and 5 more if you can sing or hum the next line.

• News: 2 points
Bonus: 5 extra points if the player can explain what the news story is about.

• Foreign Language: 3 points
Bonus: An extra 3 points if you can name the language.

• Ads: 3 points
Bonus: 5 points if you've ever bought the product.

• Classical Music: 4 points

• A Jingle: 5 points
Bonus: 10 points for singing the whole jingle yourself.

• A Weather Report: 5 points

• Sports Game: 5 points

• Call-in Show: 5 points
Bonus: 10 extra points if you can give an instant opinion on the topic.

• Traffic Report: 5 points

Once you've learned how to play the basic version of "Tuned In," try these variations:

Radio Bingo: Each player has his or her own piece of paper with a list of all of the categories shown on the previous page. When a player tunes in to one of the categories, he or she can cross it off his or her list.

The winner is the first person to cross off each of the categories. He or she can then shout, "I'm tuned in!"

In a Spin: Before play begins, draw a large circle on a piece of paper, and divide it into ten segments.

Write the name of one category in each of the sections.

Then using a pen as a spinner, one player spins to select the "instant loser" category.

Now, wearing a blindfold, take turns choosing a station. If a player chooses a station that is broadcasting the instant loser program, he or she is automatically out of the game.

Continue until only one person remains.

Make a Button Yo-yo

You can create a nifty, personalized yo-yo with just two large coat buttons (each should be at least 1 inch wide) and some extra-strong thread.

Cut 20 inches of thread and, holding the buttons back-to-back, lace the thread back and forth between all of the holes. Keep going until the buttons are securely tied together with a slight gap between them.

Push the thread through one of the holes and pull it out between the two buttons. Loop it three times around the cotton core, then knot it securely on itself.

Tie a loop in the other end of the thread that is large enough for you to slip your middle finger through. If you are right-handed, use the middle finger of your right hand.

Wind the thread of your yo-yo around the core until it is wound all the way up to the loop and you can hold the yo-yo in your palm.

LET'S GO AND YO-YO

Flip your fingers down and let the yo-yo roll off them. As it falls, turn your hand over, jerk the thread, and snatch the yo-yo as it comes back up.

Breathtaking Ball Spinning

Find out who can master this ball trick first, and who can achieve the longest spin.

Place the ball on your upturned palm, with your arm extended and slightly bent at the elbow. Practice flicking the ball about 2 1/2 inches into the air with a pat of your hand. Try putting some spin on the ball by rotating your wrist with a counterclockwise flick if you are right-handed. (If you are left-handed, rotate your wrist clockwise.)

When you can do this confidently, as the ball leaves your hand, point your index finger up and let the ball land directly on it. (Practice so you make contact at the center of the ball.) The more spin you put on the ball as it goes up, the faster and longer it will spin.

If you're getting really good, try flicking it up from your fingertip to increase the spin and then catch it again. Do this correctly and the ball will look weightless.

Cook Up Some Spooky Food

Whether it's Halloween or just a boring day that needs spooking up, conjure up these ghoulish dishes.

MONSTER'S EGGS

You will need:

- 6 cooking apples • an apple corer • ovenproof dish
  - 1/4 cup boiling water • brown sugar • butter
- kitchen tongs • maple syrup • canned whipped cream
  - a handful of washed raspberries or blueberries

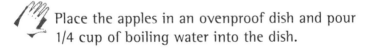

Preheat the oven to 350°F. Then wash the apples and remove the cores with an apple corer.

Place the apples in an ovenproof dish and pour 1/4 cup of boiling water into the dish.

Pour several teaspoonfuls of brown sugar into the hole in the middle of each apple and seal them with a bit of butter.

Cook the apples for about 35 to 40 minutes before removing them. They should be soft but not collapsing. Now transfer them to a tray using the tongs. Be careful not burn yourself.

Here's the fun bit. Trickle a spoonful of maple syrup over the top of each apple. Then squirt whipped cream into the center of each one. The cream will swell up and ooze over the top like something from a horror movie, and that's when you scatter the berries over the bubbling cream.

Now shriek, "Aaarghh. They're hatching!" and serve!

Tip from Dad: To create some creepy cracks in the eggs, Dad can make some vertical cuts in the sides of the apples when they come out of the oven.

HANDS OF THE UNDEAD

All you need for this is some Jell-O, a pair of rubber gloves, and a rubber band.

Mix up a bowl of Jell-O using the method suggested on the package. Lime Jell-O is a good choice.

Wash the gloves inside and out. Then carefully hold each glove at the wrist with the fingers pointing down and pour in the Jell-O.

Tightly tie the tops of each glove with rubber bands. Now place each hand in the freezer. Leave them overnight so that they freeze solid.

Now take the frozen hands out of the freezer and run them under cold water for a few seconds.

 Slowly remove the gloves by using scissors to cut the wrist of the gloves away from the Jell-O.

When the hands are free at the wrists, slowly cut away the fingers of the glove, being very careful not to snap the icy fingers off.

 Put the hands in the fridge to defrost. When they are soft enough to eat, grab some spoons and dig in.

The Saltine Challenge

Challenge each other to the ultimate snacking test. All you need are six saltines and a stopwatch, plus a lot of determination. Dad might be able to eat more food in one sitting than anyone else in the family, but will he be able to take on this challenge?

Face each other with six saltines per person close at hand. Stare into your opponent's eyes to try to freak him or her out before you start.

THE RULES

- Players are up against the clock, with just one minute to consume all six saltines.

- Contestants are not allowed to drink any water during their minute, but they can have a glass ready for their recovery once the minute is up.

WATER, WATER!

It might not look like a lot of food to chomp on — the first saltine might seem supereasy and be on its way to your stomach in moments — but just see how the rest go down.

Most people will find that their mouths simply can't produce enough saliva to allow them to swallow all six saltines.

Give it a try — you'll need that glass of water.

Make an Underwater Viewer

Wouldn't it be great to see more clearly into ponds and tide pools? Here's a simple viewer you can make to explore underwater.

You will need:

• a craft knife • a sheet of clear plastic • a stiff cardboard tube that is open at both ends • duct tape

Using a sharp craft knife, cut a circle of clear plastic that fits snugly over one end of your tube – like the lens of a telescope.

Wrap a strip of duct tape around the end of the tube, overlapping the plastic slightly. Fold it down over the edge of the plastic to secure it. Keep adding tape until you are confident that your telescope is watertight.

Next, wrap duct tape up and over the whole of your tube to waterproof it.

When you hold the open end of the tube up to your eye, you should be able to see through it clearly.

Now take your telescope on a tide-pooling or pond-life expedition and see what you can spot.

Submerge the plastic end of your viewer. Move it around slowly so as not to scare away the wildlife you are watching. If the water isn't too murky, you'll be able to see well.

Tip from Dad: Why not make a list of things that you should be able to spot in the pool or pond you are exploring? The first player to cross off everything on his or her list shouts, "Bingo!"

Make a Dancing Puppet

Here's how to make a peanut puppet.

You will need:

• a long darning needle • a spool of strong thread • a thimble • a bag of peanuts, still in their shells • 2 Popsicle sticks • paint and brushes

Start by threading the nuts together to make your dancing puppet. You will need to thread 28 inches of strong thread through the needle. Use it double thickness to make it stronger. Tie a fat knot 1 1/2 inches from one end and, using a thimble, push the needle right through one nut lengthwise (the belly of your puppet) from bottom to top. Tie a knot above the nut to keep it in place.

Make another knot just above the body. Thread a second nut on to your needle to make your puppet's head. Knot the thread above the nut, and leave the long end trailing.

Using another length of thread, push the needle through the back of the body nut at the shoulder and out to the side where the arm will start. Thread on two nuts and repeat on the other side.

Tie a knot before and after each nut, always leaving a slight gap. Leave the long ends trailing.

Repeat this process to make the legs, but use 35-inch lengths of thread double thickness. Leave the thread at the end of each leg hanging.

Bind the Popsicle sticks together with thread to make a cross-shape. Attach the head to the middle of the cross.

Attach each arm to different ends of one stick and each leg to different ends of the other.

 Use paint to draw on your puppet's clothes, and give him or her a cheerful face. Why not make a Wild West bandit with a scowl and a drooping yarn mustache?

Now practice making your puppet pal kick and whirl.

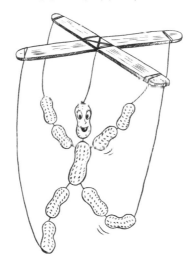

Put on a Magic Show

Stage a magic show for your family and friends, and you'll have them gasping in awe at your magical powers. The great thing is that you can take turns being the magician, or the magician's assistant. Just make sure you practice the tricks thoroughly before you perform them in front of your audience. You don't want to be booed off stage!

MYSTICAL MAGIC EIGHTS

Here's a great card trick that will convince your audience you can read minds. You need any seven playing cards and the 8 of clubs, a blindfold, and the help of a volunteer from the audience who doesn't know how the trick works.

One of you will be the magician, and the other one will be the magician's assistant.

The magician deals out the eight cards, faceup on a table, so that they are arranged in the same pattern as the eight clubs on the 8 of clubs card.

Then the assistant ties a blindfold over the magician's eyes.

The assistant asks for a volunteer from the audience and invites him or her to come up and select one of the eight cards, and show it to the audience. The volunteer then puts the card back in its place. All this is done in complete silence so the magician cannot possibly guess the card.

The magician removes the blindfold. The assistant points, seemingly at random, to the cards on the table. When the assistant points at the volunteer's chosen card, the magician shouts, "I feel a strong vibe telling me that is your card." And it is!

WHAT'S THE SECRET?

To make this trick work, the assistant indicates to the magician which card was chosen in a very simple way. Before pointing to the chosen card, the assistant points a finger at the 8 of clubs. He or she carefully only touches one of the clubs on the face of the card. The one touched corresponds to the position of the chosen card in the layout of the eight cards. For example, if the ace was the chosen card, the magician would point to the club circled below on the 8 of clubs.

A CRAFTY CARD TRICK

For the next trick, reverse roles — so that the magician is now the assistant and the assistant the magician.

The magician holds a pack of cards facedown and shows the audience what they think is the card on the top of the pack.

Instead of lifting just the top card, the magician picks up the first and second card at the same time — hiding the top card behind the second. (It is easier to lift the two cards at once if, before the performance, you have bent them slightly. In private, practice lifting the cards smoothly and confidently.)

After the magician has shown the audience what is, in fact, the second card, he or she replaces both cards on top of the pack.

The magician holds out the deck of cards and the assistant takes the top card and slips it into the middle of the pack while telling the audience, "I am placing the top card in the middle of the pack."

The card that the audience was shown is now on the top of the pack.

The magician taps the pack and says, "Abracadabra!"

The magician's assistant then shows the audience the top card and they marvel in amazement, believing the card that they saw placed in the middle of the pack has magically returned to the top.

Create a Magic Wheel

Back in Victorian times, there weren't any DVDs or computer games. A zoetrope, or magic wheel, was the nearest thing to TV. Here's how to make one of your own.

You will need:

• a pair of compasses • a piece of cardboard (10 inches by 10 inches) • a pair of scissors • a large sheet of colored paper (at least 28 inches by 9 inches) • a ruler • glue • tape • felt-tip pens • a strip of white paper (28 inches by 2 inches) • two 12-inch-long dowels • a piece of string 2 yards long

 Use a pair of compasses to draw a circle on the cardboard 8 inches in diameter. Cut the circle out.

Take the colored paper and cut three strips 28 inches in length. Make one strip 2 inches wide, one 3 inches wide, and one 4 inches wide.

Take the 4-inch-wide strip and cut it into fifteen sections — each 1 1/2 inches wide. Firmly glue the short edges of the strips along the length of the 3-inch-wide strip, leaving a gap of 1/4 inch between each strip. You should have a short gap at the end.

Now take the 2-inch-wide strip, and glue it securely along the top of the sections. This will be your viewing wheel.

With the 3-inch strip at the bottom, cut 1/2-inch notches along the lower edge. Curve your viewing wheel around the cardboard circle, folding the notches over. Use tape and glue 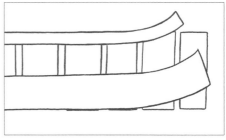 to fix the circle in place. You will also need to tape the top strip to complete the cylinder.

Take the strip of white paper that is 28 inches by 2 1/2 inches. This will make your movie-sequence strip.

Draw fifteen figures, evenly spaced along the strip. Make each picture slightly different — if you were showing a man running, his arms and legs would be in a slightly different position in each picture. Slide this picture strip inside the slatted frame and push it back against the frame so it runs all the way around, like wallpaper.

Pierce two holes, opposite each other, in the top of the paper frame and slide one of the dowels through both holes. Do the same with the other rod, fractionally lower

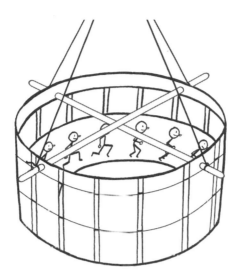

and at right angles to the first. The two rods will form a cross in the middle.

Cut four lengths of string, 20 inches each. Tie a piece to each end of the dowels. Bring the four ends to the middle of the wheel and tie them together.

Suspend the magic wheel by holding the ends of the string in one hand. Now twist the wheel in the opposite direction to the running character. Let go of the wheel and peek through the slats as it spins. Watch as your little figure comes to life! Now spin the wheel in the opposite direction so the character runs backward and the strings untangle.

Alternative ideas for animations that will work well in your zoetrope are jumping fish and bouncing balls. Keep your sequences simple for the best result.

Become a Knight

Knights of old proudly wore their family's coat of arms on their shield during jousting matches. Here's how to create some decorations that include your own family's coat of arms.

You will need:

• felt-tip pens • a piece of white cardboard at least 16 inches by 20 inches • a ruler • scissors • string • large sheets of colored paper in at least two colors • glue • masking tape

Draw a shield shape on the white cardboard, 14 inches wide and 18 inches long. Use a ruler to draw two lines 2 inches apart across the middle of the shield. Start the first line about 8 inches down from the top.

Now use a pair of scissors to cut out your shield.

SYMBOLS OF THE KNIGHT

 Dream up two designs that symbolize your family. For example, if your last name is Smith, you could draw a horseshoe in the top half of the shield. If it is Mann, you could draw a man. If there's an artist in the family, you could try drawing a palette with a brush, or you could use Dad's occupation for inspiration.

For the bottom half of the shield, choose a design inspired by an activity you enjoy together. For example, draw waves if you love visiting the beach, a baseball bat or soccer ball if you are sports fans, or a castle if you love visiting historic places.

To finish off your coat of arms, shade the three sections of the shield in different colors. How about red in the top section, green at the bottom, and yellow in the stripe?

Measure a length of string that will span the room you want to hang the shield across. Cut it just long enough so that it hangs down in a gentle arc. Pierce a hole in the top two corners of your shield and thread the shield onto the string, pulling it into the middle.

TIME TO ADD SOME DECORATIONS

No knight's debut would be complete without lots of multicolored flags.

Take some sheets of colored paper that match the colors on your shield and cut them into strips, 12 inches by 6 inches.

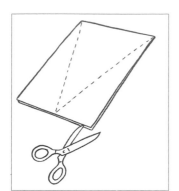

Fold the strips in half lengthwise and cut a V-shape from the open base to form a flag. Repeat with different colors of paper.

Open out the folded shapes and put a thin line of glue on the inside of the folds before gluing the flags onto your string.

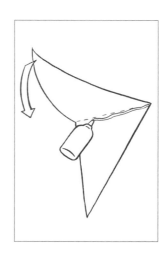

Add more flags side-by-side along your shield decoration until the string is full. Then hang it across the room, securing the ends with masking tape.

Congratulations. You have been knighted!

Create Your Own Solar System

Here's your chance to create a whole solar system of your own — one that's tiny enough to fit in your house!

You will need:

• poster paints and brushes • 5 tennis balls • a sheet of white cardboard • a craft knife • duct tape • 5 Ping-Pong balls • three 3-foot-long wooden sticks • a long darning needle • a ball of yarn • hooks

Use your paints to transform the tennis balls into planets. Paint them different colors — one could have swirls of red to show electrical storms battering the planet, and one could have clouds and continents. Go crazy — it's your solar system.

Why not cut out a ring of cardboard and push it over one of the balls to represent rings (like those that circle Saturn in our own solar system)? Secure the cardboard with duct tape and spatter the ball and the ring with paint dots.

Paint one tennis ball bright orange, because this will be the star at the center of your solar system.

Now make some smaller planets from the Ping-Pong balls.

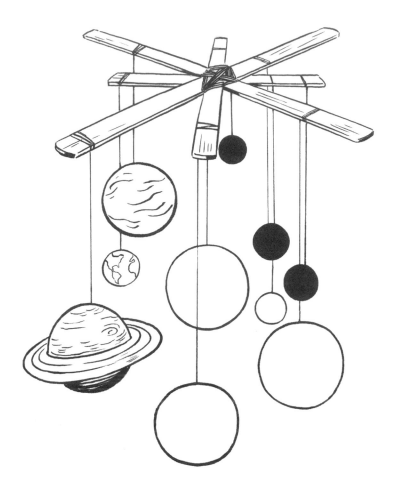

Again, paint them exactly as you like, making each one different.

 **GET MOBILE**

To make the frame of your mobile, cut one of the 3-foot-long sticks in half.

Then use some yarn to bind the two 20-inch lengths together — into the shape of a cross.

Make another cross using the other 3-foot-long stick.

Then bind the two crosses together into an eight-pointed star (as shown in the picture opposite). This is the frame on which your solar system will be suspended.

Next, you need to attach the planets to the frame. Thread a length of yarn through a long darning needle and tie a big knot in the end. Push the needle through a Ping-Pong ball and tie it to one of the sticks. Repeat for the other four Ping-Pong balls.

To add the tennis balls to your frame, screw a hook into each ball. Attach a length of yarn to each hook and suspend the tennis balls from the sticks of your frame.

Hang the fifth orange tennis ball that is your star from the middle of the mobile's frame, where the sticks cross. This star forms the center of your solar system — like the sun sits at the center of our solar system.

Hang your mobile from the ceiling and push the planets around until the whole structure balances. Then stand back and admire your creation.

Your Five Minutes of Fame

Why not play a great game called Botticelli? It's perfect for two or more players and will bring a touch of star quality to long, boring car trips.

For each round, one person is the chooser and the rest are questioners. The chooser thinks of a famous person (be fair, make sure it is one that all players will have heard of). The chooser then tells the other players the first letter of the celebrity's last name. For example, if the chooser picked Christian Bale, they would announce that the last name began with the letter *B*.

Now the other players have to think of a famous person whose last name begins with the right letter. One questioner might guess that the celebrity was David Beckham, another might guess Jack Black.

The player sitting on the right hand of the chooser takes the first turn, and asks the chooser a question to find out if the player guessed correctly. He or she might ask "Are you a British soccer star who now plays in California?"

The chooser must try to figure out who the questioner is thinking of. He or she might say, "No, I'm not David Beckham." If the chooser has guessed correctly, it is the next player on his or her right's turn to ask a question. However, if the chooser fails to guess correctly, the questioner reveals the name of the celebrity. In return, he or she gets to ask the chooser a direct question, such as "Are you male?" The chooser can only answer yes or no.

Each time the answer is yes, the guesser is allowed to ask another question, until he or she can guess the identity of the celebrity or until he or she asks a question that receives the answer no.

If a guesser thinks they know the identity of the chooser's celebrity they must ask a question – for example, "Are you Christian Bale?"

The person who guesses correctly is the chooser in the next round.

WHY IS IT CALLED BOTTICELLI?

This game is named after Sandro Botticelli because, as a rule of thumb, the stars that players choose should never be more obscure than him. You may ask – who was Sandro Botticelli? Well, he was an Italian painter, but this demonstrates that choosers should only pick well-known celebrities about whom they know something.

Marble Madness

People have been playing marbles for centuries (even before your dad was a boy).

To shoot a marble, bend your index finger into a U-shape and place the second knuckle on the ground. Rest a marble in the U-shape of the bent index finger. Use your thumb to flick the marble off your finger.

Here are some great marble games.

MONEY MARKSMAN

One player places a marble on a coin. The other players attempt to knock it off. Those who miss lose their marbles. The player who manages to do it wins the coin!

SPANNERS

One player, the placer, shoots a marble along the ground. The second player then shoots a marble, and it must land within a hand's span of the first marble. If the second player is successful, he or she pockets the first marble and the game begins again, with the winner as the placer. If they miss, a third player takes a turn trying to put a marble within a hand's span of the second shot, and pockets all the marbles if successful.

THREE HOLES

Find a flat area of earth without any grass. Scoop out three holes in the ground using a sharp stone, stick, or trowel. Players take turns trying to land marbles in all three holes, one after the other. If a marble hits another marble and sinks it into a hole, it still counts as "on-target."

The first player to hole three marbles in three shots wins.

LAG OUT

Place a marble near a wall. Players take turns bouncing marbles off the wall, trying to hit the placed marble. As players fail, there will be more marbles to hit.

Any player who hits a marble can retrieve his or her marble and choose one other. Keep playing until someone has won all the marbles or all the marbles are on the ground and nobody has won.

Hold a Golden Goal Competition

Hold your very own golden goal
competition to see who can score the most
penalties with ten attempts.

Ideally, walk to a nearby park that has a soccer field and
a goal. If that's not an option, draw a rectangle on an
outside wall with chalk to act as your goal (choose an area
of wall that is far away from any windows). If you are not
playing on grass it is a good idea to put down a mat in
front of the goal to prevent injuries to your goalie.

Draw a penalty spot on the ground about 23 feet in front
of the middle of the goal mouth.

Choose someone to be the goalkeeper and someone to be
the penalty shooter. You will also need a third person to
act as a referee.

When a penalty is taken, the goalkeeper must remain on
the goal line between the posts until the ball is kicked.
The goalie can jump up and down, wave his or her arms,

and move from side to side along the goal line in an
attempt to distract the kicker.

The kicker must outwit the goalie and get the ball into the
net with one kick. Here are some tips on how to score a
penalty:

• Place the ball on the spot. Then stomp down any loose
turf that might affect your kick.

• Make a decision about where to aim the ball, but don't
give the goalkeeper any clues (either with your eyes or
your body language) as to which area of the goal you are
aiming for. The corners marked below are the best parts of
the goal to aim for.

• You need to run up to the ball to make sure that you
have the maximum power behind your kick, so step six
paces back from the ball.

• Wait for the referee's whistle, then approach the ball at
an angle and kick it into your chosen corner.

• Goal!

Car Wash Party

If you want to raise funds and have some foamy fun at the same time, why not have a car wash party?

You will need:

- a hose • a bottle of soap suitable for washing cars
- a bucket and 2 sponges for each car washer

SPREAD THE WORD

Let your neighbors know at least a week in advance when you will be holding your car wash party. Weekends are best, since most people take their cars to work on weekdays. Why not make some flyers to put in mailboxes around your neighborhood?

SHOW ME THE MONEY

Set a price beforehand for each car wash. Don't charge too little. Find out what the local car wash costs and charge just under this amount — you are saving your customers time and trouble, after all.

ON TAP

Delegate one person to shuttle between the front door and the hot water faucet with buckets. For cold water, it's best if you can get to a faucet without traipsing back and forth through your house. Use a hose attached to an outdoor faucet if you have one.

Make sure you wear old clothes and rain boots to this party.

Now it's time to knock on doors and offer your car-washing services. Ask your customers to park their cars on the road or driveway where your hose can reach them.

WASH TIME

To get a car really clean, hose it down with cold water first. Then wash it in sections with hot, soapy sponges. Start with the roof, then the windshield and hood, before tackling the back, the sides and, finally, the hubcaps and the wheels.

Get the sponges sopping wet, and rinse them frequently. Try not to waste water or use more water than is necessary, but change the water when it becomes really dirty, or you will end up rubbing dirty sponges over the car, and that creates scratches.

HANDY HINTS

- As you finish each section, rinse it off with cold water.
- Always wash from the top down, so that muddy water isn't dripping over clean parts of the car.
- Use your sponge in long, straight strokes — a circular motion can cause swirls on the paint.
- Don't use dishwashing soap on cars as this can damage the paint.
- Use a different sponge and bucket for the wheels to avoid picking up grit from the brake pads.
- One person should stay on hose duty while the others wash. Keep switching people around so that each person takes a turn with the hose.

When you have finished your washing bonanza, count out the money you have earned and share it equally between each person. If the party has been a success, why not make it a yearly event?

COMPETITION TIME

If the party is big enough, split into two teams and hold a race to see who can wash a car faster. Award bonus points for a superclean finish.

Have a Bubble Party

Why not have a bubble-blowing competition — the bigger the bubbles the better? Here are some tips on how to make the best bubbles ever.

THE PERFECT MIX

For a great bubble mixture, add 8 tablespoons of dishwashing soap and 4 tablespoons of glycerin (available from any pharmacy) to a liter of water. Leave the mixture to stand overnight.

For extra effect, add a few drops of food coloring into the mix — but head outside if you do this, as it gets messy!

A GIANT BUBBLE MAKER

Pour your bubble mix into a large, shallow tray.

Thread two straws onto a 3-foot length of string. Tie the string in a loop between the two straws.

Holding a straw in each hand as handles, dip the loop into your bubble mix, then gently lift it out. You should have a shimmering film of bubble mix in the middle of your loop.

Hold one arm above the other and spin your whole body around in a slow circle. The mixture in the loop should billow out into a bubble.

Try twisting the straws to bring the two sides of the loop together, allowing the bubble to float free.

Tip from Dad: As you get better at this bubble-making method, increase the length of the string — you could work up to a piece that's 9 feet long.

Compete to see who can make the biggest bubble, who can make a bubble last the longest, and who can catch a bubble without letting it burst.

BUBBLE PIPE

To make a bubble pipe, use the tip of a ballpoint pen to make a small hole near the base of a styrofoam cup.

Insert the short end of a bendy straw into the hole and point the end up toward the top of the cup.

Fill the cup with enough bubble mix to cover the tip of the straw. Holding the other end of the straw level with the top of the cup, blow gently into the straw and the liquid will start to foam and bubble.

Make Paper Helicopters

Imagine having your very own helicopter that is easy to land and does not have any complicated controls. See who can make the fastest-spinning helicopter.

WHIRLY BIRD

To make one, cut a strip of paper 1 inch by 5 inches. Make a cut, 1/2-inch deep, at the midpoint of each long side.

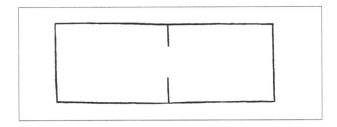

Now score a line from the bottom of each cut along the left-hand side of the cut to the edge of the paper.

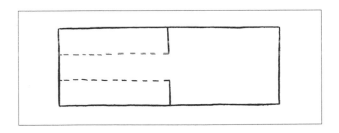

Fold the bottom section up along the score line and then fold the top section down as shown below.

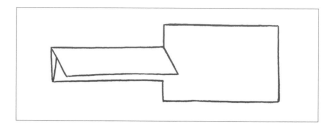

Now the left-hand side of the strip is triple thickness and 1/2-inch wide. Slip a paper clip over the end.

Make a 2-inch cut along the middle of the right-hand half. Fold the lower piece down flat. Turn the paper over and turn the other half of the strip down.

Pick up the paper and straighten out the two wider pieces, to make a T-shape.

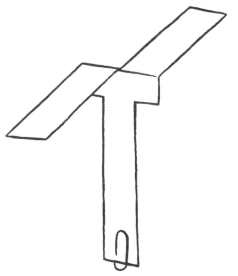

Hold the helicopter by the paper-clipped leg above your head and let it go. Watch those blades whirl!

Tip from Dad: Try adding more paper clips to make your helicopter spin and fall faster.

Carnival Fun

See who has the best aim and enjoy your very own carnival attraction.

You will need:

• 4 empty six-packs of yogurt or pudding (each of the containers must be big enough to fit a Ping-Pong ball and make sure the containers are still joined together)
• masking tape • colored acrylic paints • scissors • glue
• a large cardboard box measuring at least 12 inches by 18 inches • five Ping-Pong balls

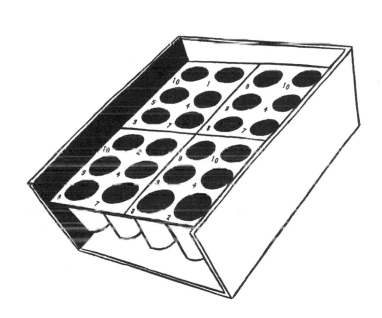

Tape the four six-packs into a rectangle (as shown in the picture on the previous page). These are your targets.

Paint the top of each six-pack a different color. Devise your own scoring system by painting a number between one and ten next to each hole. Leave the containers to dry.

Meanwhile, cut off the front and top of the cardboard box. Glue the bottoms of the yogurt containers inside the cardboard box.

To make your target board tilt toward you, put a couple of books under the end of the box.

Stand at a specified distance from your target board (younger players can be a little closer than others) and take turns seeing who can score the highest number of points by throwing five Ping-Pong balls.

Indoor And Outdoor Games

Here are some games that are great to play when you are stuck indoors, and one to play when it's sunny outside.

SARDINES

This game is hide-and-seek in reverse and it is usually played indoors.

One person hides, while everyone else counts to fifty very slowly. To stop people from rattling through the numbers too fast, you must count, "One-tyrannosaurus, two-diplodocus, three-tyrannosaurus," all the way to fifty.

Then the seekers split up and start hunting. If a seeker finds the person that is hiding, they squash in next to them in the hiding place.

The loser is the last person to find the hiding place where all the other players are squashed together like sardines in a can.

DUCK DAD GOOSE

This is another great indoor game for four players or more. Dad is the "goose" and the other players are "ducks." The ducks sit in a circle on the floor while Dad prowls around the circle.

When he touches one of the duck's shoulders, that duck has to leap to his or her feet. Both the duck and the goose sprint around the circle until they return to the empty space. The first person back to the empty space sits down. The person still standing becomes the goose.

FORTY-FORTY

This is an outdoor game. Choose a base, such as a lamppost or a tree. One person is picked to be the hunter. Let's say Dad is chosen for the first round. The object of the game is to hide while Dad counts to forty. When Dad leaves the base to start looking, the hunted need to try to get back to base without being caught.

Dad doesn't have to touch the players to catch them — he just has to see them, then run back to base and shout, "Forty-forty, I see you!" and name them.

If the hunted can run fast and beat him back to base, he or she is safe. The last person to be caught is the next hunter.

Treat your family to something AMAZING!

The Family Book

AMAZING THINGS TO DO **TOGETHER**

- OPTICAL ILLUSIONS AND MAGIC TRICKS
- MIND-BOGGLING PUZZLES AND RIDDLES
- UNIQUE ARTS AND CRAFTS

And more!

SCHOLASTIC

www.scholastic.com

FAMBOOK1